CHRISTMAS HOLIDAY
HOUSE MOUSES
LINE ART PATTERNS
by Annie Lang

Make it a Christmas Holiday season to remember with all the whimsical House Mouses you'll happily discover within the pages in this festive publication. Choose from dozens of mix and match holiday themed mouse characters and designs to create your own Christmas magic!

Simply trace the design and then transfer the image onto your project surface to make outstanding personalized items with professional results every time.

Transferring the linework designs

Trace the design of your choice with pencil and tracing paper. Place transfer paper under the tracing paper and place onto your selected surface. Hold in place with tape if necessary. Retrace over the linework to transfer the design onto the project. For fabrics, trace the design, flip the pattern over and retrace the lines using a fabric transfer pen. Follow manufacturer's direction to iron the design onto your chosen fabric item.

Color or paint these designs with

Craft paints, watercolors, markers, coloring pencils, chalks, inks, fabric pens, paint pens, or crayons

These designs are great for

Home Dec Items like furniture, cabinets, accent items, walls, lamps, glassware, kitchen accessories, office and desk items, bathroom accents, cabinets, patio pots and outdoor items, etc.
Fabric and wearable items like t-shirts, sweatshirts, aprons, canvas shoes, totes, quilting squares, table linens and napkins, window and shower curtains, pillows, etc.
Paper Craft Projects like greeting cards, scrap page elements, tags, labels, stationery items, ornaments, gift bags, etc.

For more ideas and designer tips, please visit my Blog at

http://annielang-anniethingspossible.blogspot.com/
My Pinterest Board at http://www.pinterest.com/anniethings/
or my Facebook Page at
http://www.facebook.com/anniethingspossible

Annie Lang's
Christmas Holiday
House Mouses
Copyright (C) Annie Lang
Christmas
♥ HUGS
Christmas
♥ HUGS

Annie Lang's

Christmas Holiday House Mouses

Annie Lang's
Christmas
Holiday
House
Mouses

Annie Lang's
Christmas Holiday
House Mouses
Copyright (C) Annie Lang

Merry ChristMouse

Merry ChristMouse

Annie Lang's
**Christmas Holiday
House Mouses**

Annie Lang's
Christmas Holiday
House Mouses
Copyright (C) Annie Lang

Annie Lang's
Christmas Holiday
House Mouses
Copyright (C) Annie Lang

Copyright (C) Annie Lang
Annie Lang's
Christmas Holiday
House Mouses

Annie Lang's
Christmas Holiday
House Mouses
Copyright (C) Annie Lang

Annie Lang's
Christmas Holiday
House Mouses
Copyright (C) Annie Lang

Annie Lang's
Christmas Holiday
House Mouses
Copyright (C) Annie Lang

Copyright (C) Annie Lang
Annie Lang's
Christmas Holiday
House Mouses

Annie Lang's
Christmas Holiday
House Mouses

Copyright (C) Annie Lang

Annie Lang's
Christmas Holiday House Mouses

Annie Lang's

Christmas Holiday
House Mouses

Annie Lang's
***Christmas Holiday
House Mouses***

Annie Lang's
Christmas Holiday
House Mouses

Annie Lang's *Christmas Holiday House Mouses*

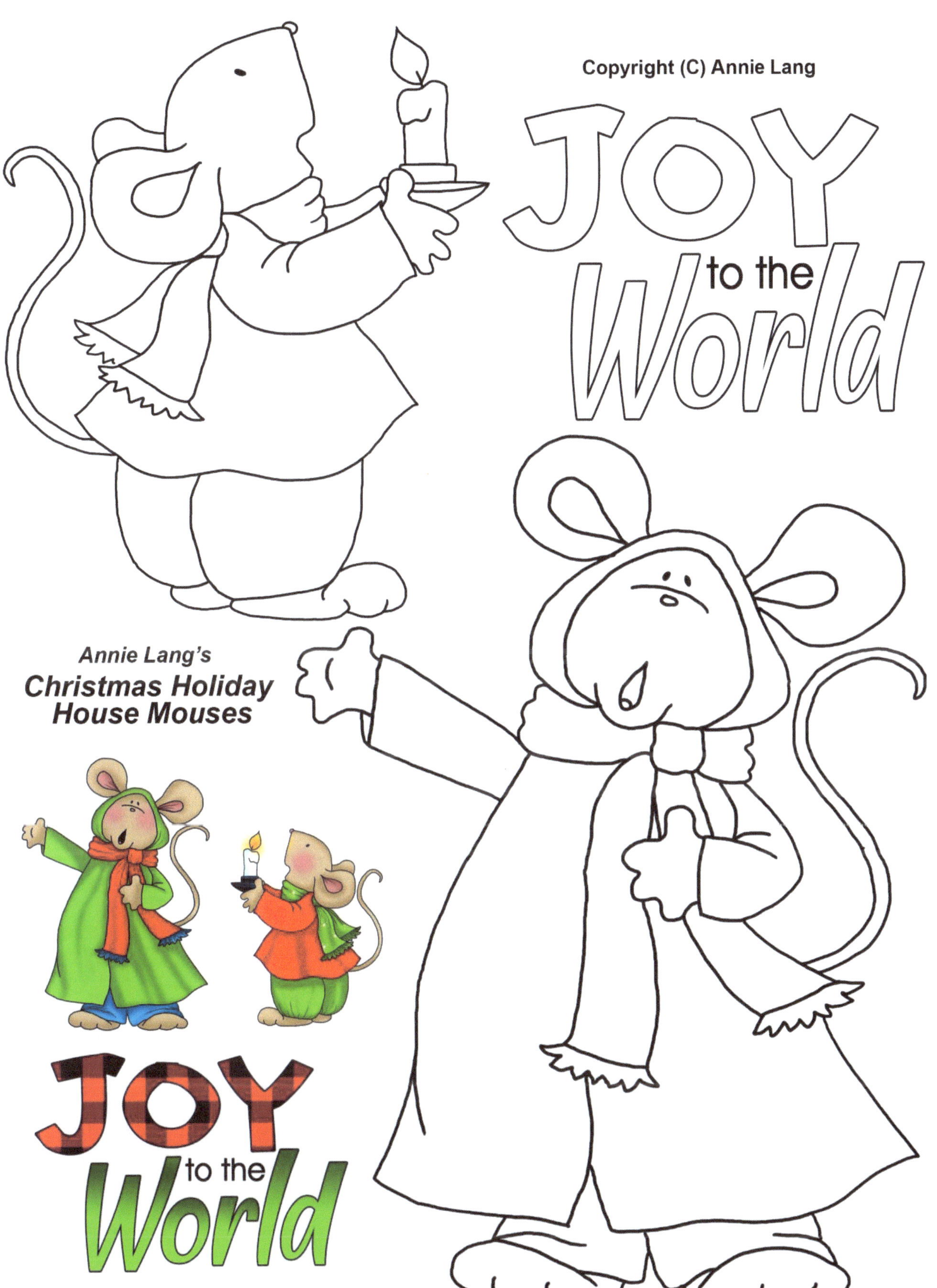

Copyright (C) Annie Lang
JOY to the World
Annie Lang's
Christmas Holiday House Mouses
JOY to the World

Annie Lang's
Christmas Holiday
House Mouses
it's the most Wonderful time of the Year
Copyright (C) Annie Lang

Copyright (C) Annie Lang
Annie Lang's
Christmas Holiday
House Mouses
it's the most Wonderful time of the year

Annie Lang's
Christmas Holiday
House Mouses
Copyright (C) Annie Lang

Annie Lang's

*Christmas Holiday
House Mouses*

Fa-la-la-la-la-la-la-la-la

Fa-la-la-la-la-la-la-la

Copyright (C) Annie Lang

Annie Lang's
Christmas Holiday
House Mouses

Annie Lang's
Christmas Holiday
House Mouses

NOT A CREATURE was Stirring not even a MOUSE

Annie Lang's
Christmas Holiday House Mouses

NOT A CREATURE was Stirring not even a MOUSE

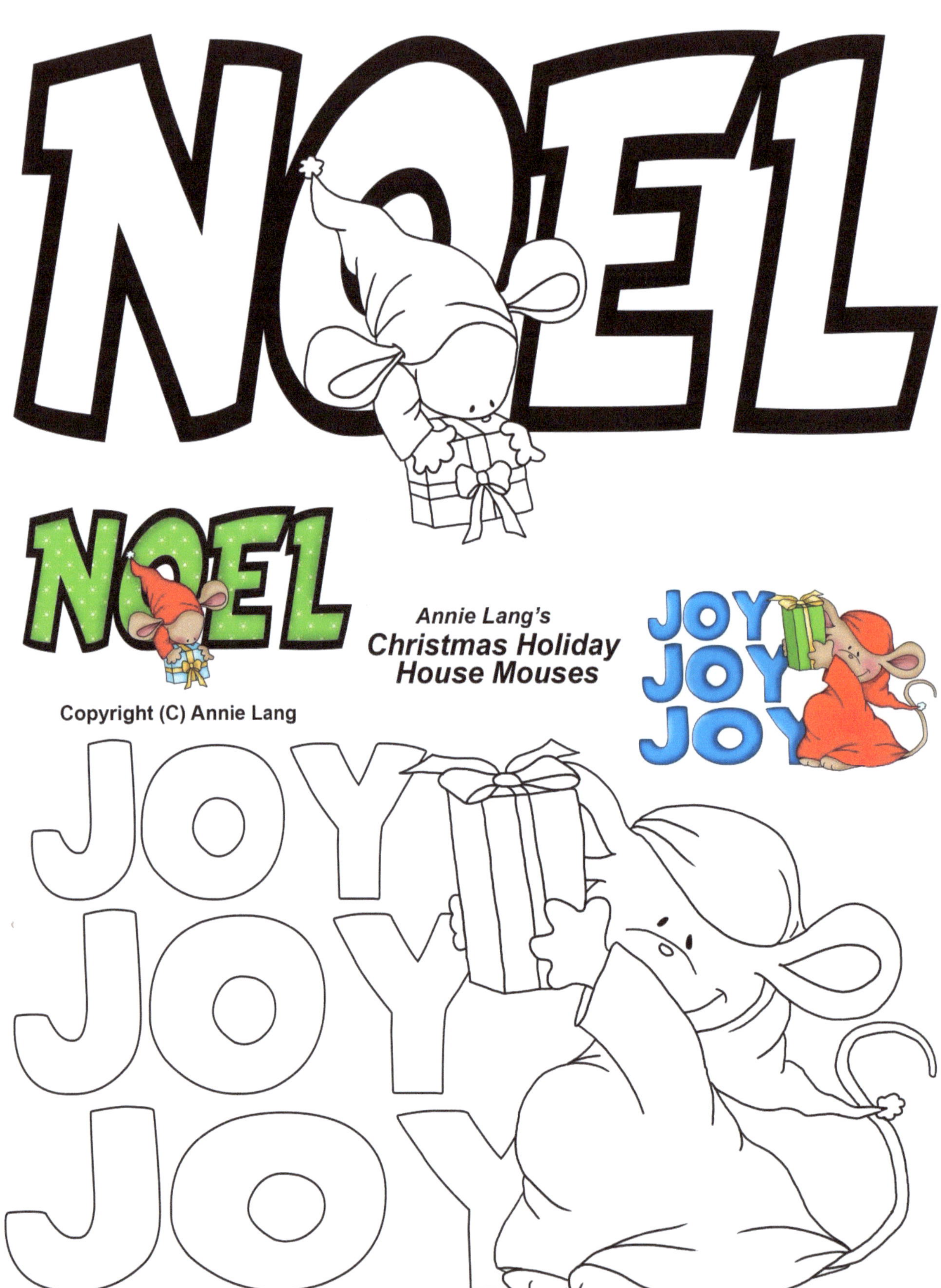

NOEL
NOEL
JOY JOY JOY
Annie Lang's
Christmas Holiday
House Mouses
Copyright (C) Annie Lang
JOY
JOY
JOY

Annie Lang's
Christmas Holiday
House Mouses

Thank you for purchasing this publication!

Find dozens of other fun titles on my
Annie Lang's Books website!

I hope you enjoyed this book and
encourage you to leave a review and share your
thoughts for other customers at Amazon.com!

To learn more about the author, get free project
ideas, see video how-to's and more, please visit
Annie Lang's BLOG at
http://annielang-anniethingspossible.blogspot.com/

www.ingramcontent.com/pod-product-compliance
Lightning Source LLC
Chambersburg PA
CBHW040208240726
48664CB00002B/872